H.O.P.E

(Hold On, Pain Ends)

By

Dominique Farmer

Copyrights © 2024 Dominique Farmer

All rights reserved. No part of this book may be reproduced, stored in a retrieval system, or transmitted in any form or by any means—electronic, mechanical, photocopying, recording, or otherwise—without prior written permission from the author, except for brief quotations in critical reviews or articles.

The scanning, uploading, and distribution of this book via the internet or any other means without the permission of the author is illegal and punishable by law. Please purchase only authorized editions and support the author's work.

ISBN: 9798875616877

I give Honor to My Lord and Savior, Jesus Christ for giving me this gift to honor You through writing.

Thank you to my beautiful children, Jelani & Jonathan for giving me time to learn and grow.

To my natural parents, Charles & Calisa Farmer, Rodney & Yalanda Ward, and my spiritual parents, Bishop C. Guy & Minister Sandra Robinson. Thank you for everything!

Dedications

I dedicate this book to Ms. Carla McCoy who asked me to teach on this during my divorce but what I didn't know was it was the title of my next book. Thank you.

Foreword

Hope can be succinctly defined as positive expectation. The hopeful person is one who is filled with expectation of a future experience that is both desirable and favorable. Subsequently, he or she can envision a positive result prior to the actual experience. And in the interim, the hopeful person remains vigilant or on the lookout for it. Such is the nature of expectation, an English word derived from the Latin verb *expectare* (as in an *exit or a way out,* and *spectator*), meaning "to be on the lookout." As a pastoral leader, I have witnessed this ability to see and expect better days despite contrarian current conditions play an essential role in transforming traumatic events, experiences, and effects into testimonies of triumph.

One of the most notable examples of the transformational power of hope that I have witnessed is the testimony of Minister Dominique Farmer. As of this writing, it has been my honor to serve as her pastor for fifteen years. Over the years, I have seen her overcome various and compounded forms of trauma. Paradoxically, and yet, I believe, providentially, I have also witnessed her spiritual formation, inclusive of the development of a powerful prayer life, prophetic gifts, prolific sermons, and inspirational writings. In a manner reminiscent of the testimony of the Biblical patriarch Joseph, God has taken those things which may have been meant for evil in her life and repurposed (or actually, *prepurposed*) them for good (Genesis 50:20; Romans 8:28). Subsequently, I believe that this book is one of the good things that have emerged from the peaks and valleys of Minister Farmer's experiences. As such, we as readers and survivors of our own tests and trials are beneficiaries of her hopeful testimony!

Finally, I would be remiss to omit the fact that hope has been known to have some powerful allies. As you prepare to read further, do so knowing that the inspired words of the apostle Paul to believers in ancient Corinth are still relevant: "And now abide faith, hope, love, these three…" I am clear about the fact that Minister Farmer's hope is inspired by her faith and love of God, family, and ministry. Therefore, I pray and trust that what she has been inspired to share will encourage and empower many others to confront and overcome life's challenges via the powers of faith, hope, and love. After all, pain ends, but faith, hope, and love abide.

CGR

Table of Contents

Dedications iii

Foreword iv

Chapter 1 1

   Why Me?

Chapter 2 6

   Realignment

Chapter 3 11

   This Hurts (Growing Pains)

Chapter 4 21

   Ugh, Not Again!

Chapter 5 25

   F, It!

Chapter 6 30

   Process is Progress

Chapter 7 40

   Where is Everyone?

Chapter 8 48

SpinnaBlock

Chapter 9 53

Introduction

Bonus Chapter.. 57

It's Time for WAR!

Acknowledgments 65

About the Author 67

Chapter 1

Why Me?

Baby, when I tell you this is a major question I tend to always ask. For me, it's always "Lord Why?" I never understood why I had to deal with some of the things I had to deal with but I was certain that it was necessary. If you were led to pick up this book then I know like myself you would love to tell Jesus, "Get somebody else to do it." Especially when these circumstances come with pain, dysfunction, and rejection. Of course, when I shared this with my close friends and family they all said I should change my question from "Why Me?" to "Why Not Me?"

Again, if you are anything like me, you think asking why not me is just straight ghetto. I am not asking Jesus, "Why not me?" Heck, I don't want it to be me at all however this is just the cross I was given to bear. Will I complain about it? Yup, I sure will. Will I trade it in for something less painful? Yup, again, I sure will. Nevertheless, I am grateful that God chose me. And because Jesus made me in his image He knows that questions of passing up this cup of suffering was an option, just like Him, I still would choose to do what is required of me.

Pain has always been and probably will always be one of the teachers of life. Pain has taught many of us what God does, what He doesn't do, what He allows, and what He does not allow. Yet, my favorite lesson from pain is who God truly is.

During some of my darkest and most painful times, I was able to learn the most about the God I served. In 2020, during COVID it was in the middle of my divorce that I learned that Jesus would never leave or forsake me. In 2021, it was in the middle of my suicidal attempt that I found out Jesus was a keeper even when I didn't want to be kept. In 2022, when I lost everything from my business to my ex-husband through death, I learned that Jesus was a comforter and the best friend a girl could ever have. In 2023, during my season of transition and redemption, I learned that God was my Father, my Husband, and truly a Friend. I remember hearing my grandmother say that if I never had a problem I would have never known Jesus could solve them. I am sure I am not the only one who has had many storms these past few years but I stand to say that in my 34 years of living, I know Jesus has and will NEVER fail. He truly is faithful.

So, no, I am not a fan of the "why not me" question. Yet, I am truly grateful that I got to experience God on a different level these past few years. Maybe it's me but how many times do we ask God in the middle of the trial, "Lord, did I do something wrong to deserve this?" Well, I am here to tell you that this trial you are in is just to showcase God's glory. Many of us have been pacing the floors and are up at night unable to sleep trying to remember if we did something wrong to deserve this very trial we are in but I am here to remind you that this is all a part of the process. Jesus implied in John 9: 4-5 that some things were necessary to do now because a time would come when no man could work. I am inclined to believe that Jesus was dismantling the spirit of procrastination. Procrastination is the arrogant assumption that God will give you another chance in the future to do something He called you to do today. Many times we put off getting closer to God or actually doing the work for a later date and time. To finally get to a place of not allowing pain to be our focus, we must allow God to put us in heart surgery.

    Jesus doesn't want us to stay in this place of pain. Although, He knows that it comes with the cost of being a Kingdom Citizen. I attended this amazing women's retreat in Scottsdale, Phoenix, given by my close friend in September 2023. When I say I left there a different person. I went for one reason but God had something else in mind for me. While there this beautiful prophetic dancer danced to "Yes" by Shekinah Glory. In the song she says, "There is more that I require of thee." During that part, I felt the Holy Spirit say clearly to me that it was time for the more but I had to release everything I was carrying. I was carrying so much baggage that I wasn't able to fully be and walk in the authenticity that God designed me to be. I was holding past hurt, past trauma, my family disappointments, my future fears, and my present all on my shoulders. I was in deep pain. Not just mental pain but it became physical pain. My back and my shoulders were always hurting but I never told anyone. For a while, I thought it was just the weight of the fact that I had a heavy chest. I was able to finally release everything in that retreat and when I came back I set boundaries that I didn't think I needed. I was finally able to say "NO" without feeling guilty. I was able to express my feelings without fear. I was able to take rejection without mentally breaking down and finally, I was able to love myself fully. Of course, I had some friends that I backed away from that called me selfish but I didn't let that stop me from fully walking in my authenticity. If my self-care was selfish to them then clearly the Lord still had some work to do with them but I was finally being obedient to God, my parents, and myself. After a while, I started seeing the fruit of me being obedient and actually spending time with God.

    I say all this to say, BABY LET GO OF THE PAIN! Give the pain to God and arise in who God called you to be. Of course, it takes time; so do not think this is an overnight process because even as I write this I am still being processed. Yet, I feel so much better than how I did when I first started this book. I literally was holding on for dear life. Nevertheless, I am a witness that if you witness to Jesus your pain, He will witness to His Father about you. Then finally you will see and experience the harvest of what God has for you. When I say harvest I do not mean prosperity all the time either. I mean your pain will officially become your push for your purpose. Hold on, Pain Ends and Your Purpose Begins.

Chapter 2

Realignment

Everyone always talks about going through a realignment process and how it always makes life make sense. Yet nobody talks about how the realignment sometimes hurts. Realignment of course is a process all by itself. I am not sure if you ever received braces but when I first received my braces I was in deep pain. The wire they placed in my mouth would pull my overbite back into place to be aligned with how my teeth are supposed to look. Having my braces on has made me feel like I was going through the same exact things my mouth was experiencing. I had moments when I was in pain after a check-in with the doctor because they added pressure and tightened the wire in my mouth. I had moments where I had to go and get a deep cleaning so that what was stuck in between my teeth could no longer stop the process of closure. I hope you hear me in the Holy Spirit. I became annoyed with the fact that I couldn't eat what I wanted anymore because it would damage the process of my teeth. I had to brush, floss, and use mouthwash twice a day and sometimes more depending on what I ate. I found a Holy Ghost filled tool called a "waterpik."

When I tell you that tool was a blessing. I was able to get some of the stubborn particles of food that were trying to hide in the cracks. Then, as soon as I thought it was close to my date for it to be removed, my orthodontist shaved my teeth down for it to be a bit smaller and then told me that I had a little more time to go. The process of realignment is just like having braces on your teeth. However, be reminded that in the end, you will have the most beautiful smile that nobody would have known about the process of braces before unless you told them. Let's not forget that even after the braces I still have to wear a retainer every day to make sure that I remain in His presence… I mean so my teeth can remain straight. Yes, the process was pretty long but be sure that when you smile you are reminded daily of what you've been through just to get here.

I love how Isaiah 61:3 says, *"To console those who mourn in Zion, To give them beauty for ashes, The oil of joy for mourning, The garment of praise for the spirit of heaviness; That they may be called trees of righteousness, The planting of the Lord, that He may be glorified."* In order to receive beauty we must first have gone through the burning to become ashes. To experience pure joy we must know what mourning feels like. To be filled with praise we must know what it's like to feel heavy and depressed. Realignment is here if you want it. Beauty is here. Joy is here. Yet it comes with realigning yourself back with Christ.

I would have never been able to write this book for you if I had not experienced deep pain. Divorce, Depression, Death, Domestic Violence, and Despair were my ashes. It was what made Dominique. However, during my process of realignment, I began to feel pressure as I became straight. I began to experience a deep cleaning and a trimming of things that were holding my process up. I used my tools, the Bible, prayer, and worship to remove the stubborn parts of me that were hiding deep down. I began to shave down unnecessary things, people, and places that were not helping my growth. And as I began to be consistent with being in God's presence I began to see and hear differently. By all means I still have a lot of growth to go through. I still have moments where I am struggling in my faith. I have moments where what I see doesn't match what God said to me and doubt begins to rise. However, I am a spiritual being living a human experience. I still have moments where the human experience wins. Yet, it may win the battle but The Holy Spirit has already won the war.

    The enemy is dirty and he does not play fair. In my season of realignment, the enemy was hijacking my dreams because he couldn't mess with me anywhere else. I worshiped 99% of the day and the little time I slept was his only option. When I say he was messing with my dreams. One morning I woke up so mad that he kept messing with my dreams. I was determined to fight back but I was going to fight God's way. I was not going to give in to his tactics and allow him to keep attacking me. Eventually, someone was going to get tired and I was determined this time it was not going to be me. So, I decided to do some research and find scriptures that I could recite and read so that I could fight back the way Ephesians 6:10-18. I knew that this round I was not going to lose because I was going to resist the devil the way the scriptures told me to. I knew God gave me strength but was I going to use the strength God gave me or was I going to keep using my own strength? God wanted me to fully depend on Him and I was determined to do that.

In Luke 9:51 it says, *"As the time approached when Jesus was to be taken up into heaven, he determined to go to Jerusalem."* I was so surprised to have read this scripture because even though Jesus knew that death was his portion; He was still determined to go to where His death was soon to happen. To me that made me understand life so much more. If Jesus was determined to complete his mission knowing death was the way then so could I. If my mission on earth included the death of self so that Jesus's light can shine through me then so be it. I now was ready to fully step into what God had for me. I was ready to fully be all God called me to be. I wanted to be in alignment with what God had for me. I was tired of settling for just the way I could do it. Going about life in my own strength was not getting me anywhere. Yet my season of realignment and my season of becoming pure meant I had to die to my impure self and what seemed comfortable in my toxic traits. I was fumbling the bag that God had given me to help heal me. Yet, I was hurting the very people that God placed in my life to help me grow. Nevertheless, I was determined to be better because I now knew better. My waterpik aka the Holy Spirit was able to get some of the stubborn demonic seeds that the enemy left within me from the past generations. The Holy Spirit was truly helping me heal. The Holy Spirit was truly helping me through a deliverance.

Realignment hurts. Realignment is hard. Realignment is scary. Realignment is frustrating. However, realignment produces beauty. Realignment produces peace. Realignment produces joy. Realignment produces stability. While I was scared of the future because of my past I knew taking this moment to realign and recommit to Jesus meant that my ending would be better than my beginning. Even the scriptures say, *"'The glory of this latter temple shall be greater than the former,' says the LORD of hosts. 'And in this place I will give peace,' says the LORD of hosts."* (Haggai 2:9) I declare and decree that peace shall be our portion, just hold on for this pain shall end.

Chapter 3

This Hurts (Growing Pains)

Lord, how much more do I have to go through just to finally heal? This has been my consistent prayer ever since my divorce. I didn't realize how much pain came with growth. Nobody ever tells you that growing up hurts. Your pride gets broken, your ego gets tossed, your confidence in yourself sometimes gets stepped on, and the Lord knows what you thought would last forever sometimes just doesn't work out. It's like the very thing you learned to survive is being ripped away from you in order to thrive in a new healthy way. What used to get you what you wanted does not work anymore. What used to help keep me afloat just wasn't the best thing to do anymore. Growth required a lot of unlearning and reprogramming. As a divorced mom, I had the privilege to send my children with other family members for what I call "Mommy Moments." Some moments after getting my kids back from some family members I had to reprogram my children to what we did in the house. At their grandparents' houses, they were able to get whatever they wanted. Yet, here my children heard the word "No" often. It wasn't that my children were being taught wrong at my parents' homes but what worked at their home just didn't work at mine. Plus, what I was teaching them was bigger than just allowing them to be children. I was teaching them how to be little people that will later grow into healthy adults. Yet, at their grandparents' homes, they were just enjoying the benefits of being grandchildren. You see what worked in one setting no longer worked in the other. What helped you survive during a single season won't help you thrive as a married individual. What helped you survive as a worker will not help you thrive as an entrepreneur. Unfortunately, the very things, ideas, tactics, coping mechanisms, and disciplines that helped you survive in your painful season will not and cannot work in your thriving season. Scripture says in Philippians 3:13-14, *"Brethren, I do not count myself to have apprehended; but one thing I do, forgetting those things which are behind and reaching forward to those things which are ahead, I press towards the goal for the prize of the upward call of God in Christ Jesus."* Sometimes those things behind you are the very things that cannot go with you into the place called forward. The prize will require you to show up fully and be ready.

I am grateful for healthy friendships because my good girlfriend, Kathy, said to me one day after crying over an argument with my significant other that this emotional rollercoaster that I kept putting myself on was unfair not just to the individual but also to me. Her words were, "These high highs and these low lows that you keep having are not healthy and this very thing will keep you from really receiving the thing you desire." I knew what she meant but because this was my coping mechanism during divorce this was all I knew. Now that I am in a new relationship this wasn't going to work. Nevermind the new relationship this was not going to work moving forward at all. Throughout my last marriage, we always had high highs but when we were low, we were low. This carried over to my divorce stage of just isolating and crying out those moments of loneliness. Also, during my divorce, I didn't really have friends who went through it all with me. I felt like as soon as the judge said it was final everything changed so my only coping mechanism was to lock myself in my dark room, stay in the bed curled up, and cry. The other option was to go to my vice of choice but after a while that became toxic too. Everyone has their vices when they are going through, drinking, drugs, eating, shopping, or having sex. Either way, the numbing from the vice never lasts long so even after the high from the vice option, crying still happened. These were my growing pains. After a while the vices ended and the prayers began. The crying never stopped but the way I cried changed. Now that I was dealing with the loss of my ex-husband and now in a relationship, those coping mechanisms started to resurface. That moment when Kathy said what she said to me I had made up my mind that yes I felt sad and yes things were not going the way I desired, but I was going to dig in and take the moment to experience the low but not stay in it. By that afternoon, I was sitting up watching Fast & Furious. If you ever suffered from depression you know sitting up in the bed instead of laying there curled up is a stepping stone. Even though I ate lunch in my bed I still ended the night reading, spending time with my children, and actually writing this chapter. What can I say, clearly that talk did something. As I sit here I know that what I have done in the past just won't work for where I am going or for where I am. My dreams require my full self and if I keep having these moments where I cannot focus or still keep going even through a rough day then I will never make it to the finish line.

This is not the first time I have had to deal with growing pains. I felt like I was always in a transition in life. I always had to change something or outgrow behaviors. The psalmist says, "*Life is filled with swift transitions.*" Swift transitions were my life. Things always happened swiftly. I either had to relearn myself in the transition or reprogram myself to survive the transition. Yet each transition required a different version of me.

When I first started writing this book I was in a place of feeling the ending of a divorce and finally feeling a bit better.

Then my ex-husband died and things began to spiral. I started to feel the pain again and feel the hurt of why me and why now? That transition left me feeling lost again, unwanted, lonely, and feeling like I was just forever going to be in this place of darkness. Even though I am still in this transition I know that there has got to be something better than this feeling. Many people talk about the pain of a relationship ending or the loss of something we thought would last. Yet nobody talks about the pain we feel when God says *"No"* or *"Wait."* That pain is a whole different level of pain. Because my earthly father and I had a rough start, my trust and outlook on my heavenly Father haven't been too pleasant. Anytime God would tell me *"No"* or *"Wait"* I would take it as him rejecting me or just not loving me. When I had to walk away from a relationship, I felt like God just didn't like me. He surrounded me around everyone in healthy and loving relationships yet I was being teased with a fraudulent relationship. How I felt about my natural father was how I felt spiritually. All my siblings are married yet I was divorced and now a "widow." Why didn't God bless me with a beautiful marriage yet? How come my siblings who got to grow up under my father's direction were in happy loving relationships yet I was struggling with finding love? I just didn't understand that process. My best friends were in beautiful relationships and I was eagerly happy for them yet deep down I was sad that I couldn't experience the same level of joy they were experiencing. I wasn't jealous, I was inspired to have my own yet it just wasn't happening for me at the same time theirs were. And of all things, God surrounded me with it. I mean it was everywhere. Family, Friends, heck even my exes were in relationships yet I was the single friend hurting and desiring marriage. As bruised as my heart was I still had a mustard seed of faith that one day I too would experience romantic love and maybe one day marriage again. However, at the moment I was frustrated and angry that God was basically teasing me and making me feel alone. I didn't understand why I had to wait and why the season of release was surrounding me. It started to make me feel all alone again. These feelings were practically normal for me. I was raised as an only child so feeling alone was my normalcy. I never felt connected to anyone. Which is why I always longed for companionship. I always desired a connection. What I didn't know was that my desire to connect was deeper than just companionship but it was a desire to connect more with our Heavenly Father. My spirit was hungry for more of its Creator. My spirit wanted my entire being to be in alignment with who created us. Yet, because I was still developing a connection with my natural father, connecting with my spiritual father was pretty much identical. What I didn't realize was my Heavenly Father really could help with my relationship with my natural father and even the partnerships I desired. However, this requires me to fully trust but because I was so bruised in previous relationships my trust for others was very slim, especially with male figures.

    I had finally gotten into a beautiful relationship and now God wanted me to release it to Him but I just couldn't see that happening. Yet, the more I tried to control it the messier it became. I had no choice but to release this relationship to God. Yet because I never dealt with my anger with God on why he never healed my first marriage or why I had to bury my children's father; releasing another relationship into His hands just wasn't easy. I wanted to hold onto it and control it because I wanted to make sure everything would go as He had shown me in the dream. Funny, right? I, with limited power, wanted to make sure the relationship that God, who has all the power, gave me would go as the dream He gave me. Does that make any sense? You weren't supposed to say NO that loud. I knew it didn't make sense at the time, yet I was trying to gain some type of control. My trauma response was to fight for control because in my mind having some type of control meant I would guarantee some type of safety for myself. Yet if you know, anytime a woman tries to control a man it never goes right and it definitely is perversion. Which means what I was actually doing was perverting the blessing God gave me. Which meant after a while the very thing I was trying to prevent happening would happen. My desire wasn't to lose the relationship but eventually, if I didn't release my control God would snatch it anyway so that I would not mess up another soul because of my perversion. So, here I am, having to make a choice, either give God complete control to save the relationship or keep my control and damage the relationship and possibly cause more heartbreak to myself and to him. My fear of releasing the relationship to God was that it did not guarantee that he and I would stay together. However, it did guarantee that nobody would be damaged because when we place items in God's hands we do know that He wouldn't damage us but more so bless us. His scripture does say in Jeremiah 29:11, *"For I know the thoughts that I think towards you, says the Lord, thoughts of peace and not of evil, to give you a future and a hope."* So, we know God's plan is to bless and prosper us but the fear of losing another person was just crippling me. In my life, the majority of my pain was because of losing someone or something. I had dealt with so much grief that loss had become my normal and holding on was my trauma response. I had never wanted anyone to feel the pain I had felt with leaving or abandoning them. However, holding on to something that caused more pain for me and someone else because of my fear was selfish. Because I was a giver at heart, being selfish isn't in my nature. I found myself giving God control but also asking God every day if everything was going to be okay. I felt like I was in an emotional surgical procedure.

I needed reassurance that God had my back and that He really had my best interest at heart. I just knew this was going to be a hard process. Not only was I checking in with God, but I was checking in with my significant other and checking to see if I was still on the outs with him. He was so cold with me that I eventually felt like giving up. I felt there was no point in trying anymore and that maybe the dream God showed me was just that, a dream. I started to not see hope.

Then this one particular day after coming home from work and him shutting my idea of building a business with him, my friend called me and she was crying about not having hope that her son's birthday party was going to be okay. It was in that moment of me ministering to her to hold on and that things were going to work out when I heard God also ministering to me. I found myself quoting to her Galatians 6:9, *"Let us not become weary in doing good, for at the proper time we will reap a harvest if we do not give up."* Babbbbyyy, when I tell you I almost broke down and cried. I was utterly annoyed that He was being so cold to me, my dream was fading, and I felt that I was doing good for absolutely no reason. Even though my doing good had absolutely nothing to do with him He was still the motivation. I had finally made up my mind that the only way this would work was if I was open and honest about myself and where I was in this process. I had finally become vulnerable but because it was after a bad situation my vulnerability didn't matter at the time with him. I had no choice but to cry out to God for assistance. It was in God's word that gave me strength to fight for my peace of mind and it gave me a second wind to finish this race to wholeness. Whether it was with him or not. Of course, at the moment I wanted it to be with him. Yet, I knew that if it didn't get better with him, then God clearly had better for me. What I did know for sure was that eventually somehow, somewhere this pain I was feeling would end. It had to because God promised.

Chapter 4

Ugh, Not Again!

This could not be real. How could this really be happening? I just finally got to the place where I was okay with the divorce now you mean to tell me that he's gone. We just got comfortable with the lifestyle of him answering the phone and him here on the holidays and important things. I just saw him, Monday! These were all the thoughts that went through my head when I sat on the floor in tears screaming because my first love had died. I didn't know what to think, say, or even feel. We have kids that need both parents. I asked God not to make me a single parent and I already was dealing with that as a divorced mom but now their father was really gone. I couldn't understand why? Why my family? Why me?!!!

We have officially gone through more than some others. I was 32 and my little family alone has dealt with depression, suicidal attempts, addiction, imprisonment, domestic violence, divorce, and now death. Not just any death but a major part of our family. I lost my first love, my kids lost their father. While I had already lost him as a husband due to divorce, I just knew he would be a part of my life for the remainder of it. I just knew I would have to fuss him out later in life about me finally marrying someone else and having to have a blended family.

I was not ready to face this battle of raising my kids physically alone. I was so angry with him for leaving us for good this time. How could the boy that I grew up with who later became my husband, the father of my children leave me like this? We were best friends, even when our divorce took a toll on our friendship our love for one another never died. We shared so many important parts of each other's life. I could not imagine spending the remainder of my life without him. Even when I became a minister, while he wasn't there physically, He sent me a long message telling me how proud he was of me. At this point in my life, I just knew God clearly loved putting me through grief. I had suffered so much that I was in a place of, okay, God, I give up! How much did I have to go through? I had suffered from loss since I was a child.

All I could say when I got the call of my children's father was, UGGGGHHHHH NOT AGAIN!!! From a child's loss was my portion. From losing the physical presence of my father being there to my first boyfriend being shot, to my godmother passing away while I was in transition to High School, to almost losing my life and ending up in Sheppard Pratt, to me losing friends that I thought were lifelong friends because of the call on my life, to me grieving in my marriage because it was toxic, to me losing my business and home because my husband at the time was stealing money, to me losing him to drugs which caused a divorce to now Jonathan, my covenant partner and children's father dying from a seizure due to his sickness. Grief was my portion. At this point I felt like Naomi in the Bible, *"Call me Mara, for the Almighty has dealt very bitterly with me."* (*Ruth 1:20b*) I just didn't understand why I was dealing with all this so close in time. I just didn't understand why God felt the need to give me all this. Plus I thought, "God didn't give you more than you could bear." I have no clue who decided to misquote scripture and tell this lie but it was definitely not accurate for me. However, what I realized was that God actually wanted me to lean on Him due to all the issues I was experiencing. Just like Naomi, I had to go back to where God dwelled so that I could actually be healed of all the trauma I had experienced in the past few years.

    I had to face myself and the pain I was dealing with. Yet I just wasn't ready to face myself again. I thought I had just dealt with myself during my divorce. However, God had something bigger in mind. There was more that God required from me. I thought what I gave Him was enough but God wanted more. He wanted all of me but I wasn't ready to actually give him everything. Nevertheless, I wanted God's will to be done on earth as it was in heaven for me and my family. If that meant I was going to have to submit even more the part of my fear of losing another thing. Rejection and abandonment was a coat I felt I wore comfortably but God wanted me to give Him the coat of victim and walk in Victory. Yet I was scared to be let down again. I was scared to lose again. I was scared to grieve again. God reminded me that His word said, *He has not given us a spirit of fear, but of power and of love and of a sound mind.* (2 Timothy 1:7)

Chapter 5

F, It!

Baby, when I say God has dealt me heavily with this word, FORGIVE. I thought for years that I forgave a lot but in reality, I was really just burying it... or shall I say I planted it. I had to literally uproot the seed of my bitterness. Thank God for covenant friendships because my best friend led me to her apostle who began to do counseling with me on the days I didn't have therapy. Yes, to me there is a difference. So, my therapist was there to help me with my mental state. She was my mind doctor. However, the apostle was there as my spiritual midwife. She helped me birth the healed Dominique. One particular session she had me going through a deliverance with uprooting all the hurt I felt in my life that I never forgave people about. Even though I thought I did, when we started the process I realized it still plagued me. We did this exercise of me literally crying out to God for all the hurt I blamed Him for. Yes, I blamed God for a lot of the abuse I received from others as well as the abuse I did to myself.

Many people talk about forgiving others but do we tell God that we forgive Him? I literally was hurt by God. I was angry that He allowed so much pain to happen to me. I didn't quite understand. This bitterness was damaging my outlook on God, life, my relationships, and most importantly, myself. That night literally changed my life. Even though it went over to the next day I had to take the day off because God was still uprooting seeds of rejection and abandonment in me. He was uprooting seeds of bitterness and I was finally able to really forgive God, my parents, my ex-husband, old friends, and myself. Of course, I am still walking it out but I am no longer carrying around baggage that was holding me down.

Forgiving releases you from the past trauma and expectations that you placed on yourself. Walking in true forgiveness allows you to be open for blessings that you weren't able to maintain because your bitterness toward life, love, and joy would have made you mismanage the very thing you prayed for. As I sit here and type this I am grateful for that moment because now I realize that God allowed me to release it all and finally grow in areas that I thought were just stagnant. Scripture says in 2 Corinthians 3:17, *"Now the Lord is the Spirit; and where the Spirit of the Lord is, there is liberty."* When we invite the Lord into our lives and allow Him to uproot all evil seeds that were placed in our lives through the enemy and his tactics, we enter into a level of freedom that allows us to finally flow in the Spirit of the Lord. I am grateful that forgiveness was my portion and now I am freely able to extend forgiveness just like Jesus forgave me. I love how Jesus says in Luke 6:37-38, *"Judge not, and you shall not be judged. Condemn not, and you shall not be condemned. Forgive, and you will be forgiven. Give, and it will be given to you: good measure, pressed down, shaken together, and running over will be put into your bosom. For with the same measure that you use, it will be measured back to you."* All my churchgoers thought that was just talking about money. However, it is talking about everything. Judging, Condemning, and my new favorite, Forgiving. As you give forgiveness you will get it back pressed down, shaken together, and running over. I don't know about you but I always need forgiveness. I try my hardest not to hurt people, however, every once in a while my tone or my reaction may bring harm upon someone unknowingly. Of course, it is never my intention to hurt anyone yet sometimes I just need a little forgiveness. I believe we all have some areas that we either need to forgive someone about or ask for forgiveness. As I always say, we are spiritual beings living a human experience. Jesus has not returned, which means nobody on earth, not even the over-sanctified apostle that attends your church is not perfect. We all have at least one area that God is still working on us. If we are honest it's probably more than one. Or maybe that's just me being too honest. Forgiving others allows you to release and finally be open to receive. There's this old saying that you can't receive what

God has for you if your hands are full of things that you never decided to release. That goes for those people that you never forgave. Trust me, I know forgiving someone takes time. However, you don't want to waste any more time holding on to a hurt that can eventually harm you physically or stop your growth spiritually.

For years I was angry with my father and what he had not done or didn't do. I was an adult stuck with the little girl's brain who was hurt and rejected by her father. I wasn't able to move forward. Time went past and it wasn't until I realized that He was living his life while I was still holding on to what hurt me. It wasn't until I made a decision to forgive him that I was able to start the process of healing. Now, he and I have a way better relationship than I would have ever thought would happen. I would have missed out on the opportunity to bond with my father, my bonus mother, and my siblings more with me holding onto hurt that really wasn't even my portion. Of course, making this decision came with some conversations with both sets of my parents. I had to come to grips that I was no longer going to choose them but I was finally going to choose me. I wanted a relationship with all of my parents. Not many are blessed with 2 sets of parents like I am and have a good relationship with all of them. My mother and my bonus dad were just as special to me as my dad and my bonus mom. I no longer wanted to be that Dominique who felt abandoned, rejected, and carried the spirit of an orphan. I was ready to release and forgive not just my parents but also myself. Forgiveness was and is the key to unlocking the door of restoration. You have the key, will you use it? That is the question.

Chapter 6

Process is Progress

Many days I found myself feeling like I was stagnate and nothing was progressing in my life. I felt that I was just moving way too slowly for my timing. It was one morning when I was sitting in my quiet place that I heard the words, "Don't fumble the bag!" For a minute I was confused about what bag God was talking about because at the moment my new hunny was acting funny, my money was tight, my job was annoying and my business was acting like it just didn't like me at the moment. I became so frustrated that everything was not going the way I wanted at the time I wanted. However, I had to take my hands off and allow God to be God. So many times we, with control issues, forget that we actually have no control over anything. We were given authority over things on the earth but time is not ours to control.

After much meditation and time with Jesus, I realized that the bag I was about to fumble was my purpose. Oftentimes, when things are not going our way we mishandle the bag by not focusing on carrying the bag and more so about what's in the bag. Everything in the bag was given to you because it's in alignment with your purpose. The possessions you have are all purpose-driven. The bag is a part of your purpose. We must not focus so much on what's in the bag but the purpose of carrying it. My best friend said to me one day as I described the season I was in, "Dominique, you must take your eyes off the promise and the people involved in the promise and be about the purpose!" Baby!!!! I almost lost it when she said this to me. I was filled so much with inspiration and realized that what I was really going through was a process. My character was being processed. If God was to deliver my promise to me at the moment, I would have fumbled the bag. I had to be reminded that even though I was being processed, I was still making progress. If God delivers the promise to those with poor character the individual will prematurely abort the assignment. I know I have done this plenty of times because I was not in the place to handle the weight of the bag I was carrying.

Now let's be reminded that there are bags that we should not be carrying. Some weight is meant to be cast on The Father. However, some weight the Father has designed us to carry because He anointed us to handle the assignment with grace. What normally messes us up is we look to social media and want to look like we have the bag but in reality, we haven't even picked up the bag God designed for us to carry. We are too busy trying to make sure our bag is a luxury brand or too busy trying to pick up a replica of someone else's bag. Your bag is just that… YOUR BAG! What's meant for you is custom-made just for you.

So, as I continued to pull myself out of this funk, God began to download how I could help the process and how not to fumble the bag. And because I love you so much I wanted to share these tips so that we all can cancel the assignment of the enemy and the spirit of premature death that has been knocking at our door of purpose. I have read so many millionaire mindset books and a lot of the "How to Become Successful" books and I realized that the world was making a killing off of Kingdom Principles! I felt like they basically took what belongs to us, kingdom citizens, and gave it a knockoff name. To top it off, they were selling the information back to us as if we didn't have the same information FOR FREE! The Bible is located in everyone's phone app store FOR FREE! So sorry to break it to you and I know this will hurt because it hurt my feelings too but… WE GOT PLAYED! Scripture tells us in Hosea 4:6, *"My people are destroyed for the lack of knowledge."* Let's stop allowing the spirit of ignorance to win in our lives. God has blessed us with the ability to gain wealth and I don't mean just money. It is so much bigger than just being financially free.

Keeping the bag will require us to invest in Kingdom Principles. That means studying the word of God and finding out what is offered to us. We all know the main ones that are drenched all over social media. For example, the world is always talking about manifesting. While I am not against it, if we are only manifesting what we want and not God's will we are tapping into another dimension that we are not equipped to handle. I am not just speaking from knowledge, I am also speaking from experience. During my 'lost' season, I was trying all types of things to become "something". I manifested a vehicle, some opportunities, and even money. However, I was awakened when the items I manifested came with issues that were above what I like to say, "my pay grade". The items I manifested came with issues that I couldn't afford, spirits of pride, people with spirits of jezebel, leeches, and more. Yet, God is a forgiving God and the God of another chance! Once I gave my life back to Christ (again) things began to be repossessed out of my life. Now granted, some I gave away because I knew it just wasn't it. I was grateful that He never left me stranded or abandoned but God took what was not right for me and replaced it with something better or something I was able to steward well for the season I was in. Proverbs 13:11 says, *"Wealth gained by dishonesty will be diminished, But he who fathers by labor will increase."* While you may not be a dishonest person, manifesting is the total opposite of laboring for your increase. Also, when manifesting we are asking God mainly for his permissive will and not necessarily His perfect, pleasing, or goodwill for our lives.

Investing into our kingdom principles is not just for the possessions that come with it but it's the lifestyle we are expected to live. One particular book I read explained that we were to talk and walk as if what we wanted to happen was already happening for us. I laughed when I read it because one scripture that always stuck in my mind was Romans 4:17b *"God, who give life to the dead and calls those things which do not exist as though they did."* That is the scripture where everyone says *"Speak those things that be not as though they are."* This is a kingdom principle that the world has taken and has prospered off of. I am clueless about why we as Kingdom citizens have not used the very principles that Jesus taught us, so that we could live in the abundance that He already declared was our birthright. I love how Malachi 3:10 says, *"'Bring all the tithes into the storehouse, That there may be food in My house, And try Me now in this,' says the Lord of hosts, 'If I will not open for you the windows of heaven and pour out for you such blessing that there will not be room enough to receive it.'"* There we are told of another Kingdom Principle and we hear The Lord say **"TRY ME"**. If that doesn't make you want to test it out then I don't know what will. Maybe it's me and I always have that "try it myself" personality, but that alone made me try it out and see what would happen. It reminded me of when my mother would say try me and see what happens. Obviously, that didn't always mean something good but because I wanted to know what the "see what happens" truly meant I tried it. Majority of those times I received a whopping or punishment but God says exactly what would happen if we tried His kingdom principle. He says He would open up the windows of heaven and pour blessings so much that we wouldn't have any room to receive it all. So, if giving 10% of my tithes to His house meant that He would overload me with blessings that I wouldn't have room to receive then what exactly was I waiting on? Once I saw that principle and the outcome of my trying it, I asked where His house was and can I give 15% just in case.

Not only are we to stay disciplined with investing in our Kingdom Principles but we must also stay focused. Keeping your mind on the assignment or the task at hand allows you to remain focused. To be honest, we really must keep our minds on Jesus Christ. Staying focused on Him allows us to stay focused on what is in front of us and not what's behind us. Scripture says, *"Brethren, I do not count myself to have apprehended; but one thing I do, forgetting those things which are behind and reaching forward to those things which are ahead, I press toward the goal for the prize of the upward call of God in Christ Jesus."* (Philippians 3:13-14) Staying focused on the pain does nothing for you but draws you deeper into a dark place. Yet, pressing forward allows you to move toward the future. When driving a car the only way you won't crash into the person in front of you is if you keep looking forward. However, if you keep looking into your rearview mirror instead of looking forward the entire time then you can cause more damage to not just yourself but those connected or surrounding you. Many people forget the number one rule of driving is not to stay focused for just you but also to stay focused and cognitive of your surroundings.

If you knew that there was this special tree in your garden that bears fruit, why would you put your main focus on the apples it bears and not more so on the task of caring for the tree? If making sure the tree was taken care of would result in more fruit why waste your energy on just enjoying the apples? Absolutely not a wise decision! The main focus would be watering the one tree, pruning the tree, and then later plucking the apples to eventually plant more trees to have more to invest in others. Social media has programmed us to think we need to focus on the apples and make sure we make apple pie, apple cobbler, and applesauce. They never tell you after a while if you don't focus on the task of maintaining the apple tree, eventually a drought will come and you won't have any more apples. You will use all the apples up and then run to Jesus to give you more. How fair is that when you could have just been a good steward of the apples you have? It's like we sin more so that grace will abound but that's not scripture. Apples don't just stand for money but grace, joy, relationships, your esteem, your capacity that you give out to others, your love and/or possessions, or the promise that comes with doing your purpose. When will you begin to do the planting, the pruning, and the reinvesting also known as creating boundaries? The only way out of this slump is if you are about Kingdom business. Yes, that comes with eternal reward but there are some benefits that will come to fruition here in the land of the living. The reward will not only help the pain end but it is everlasting meaning it's generational. Proverbs 13:22 states, "A good man leaves an inheritance to his children's children, but the sinner's wealth is laid up for the righteous." If you want to be the one to create generational blessings then you must stay disciplined and stay focused on the Kingdom work. I mean you are a kingdom citizen, right?

Lastly, we must learn to stay positively patient in the process. Proverbs 18:20-21 speaks of us eating the fruit and reaping a harvest from what we say out of our mouths. We can either speak and eat the fruit of life or we can reap the harvest of the death we spoke out of our mouths. As I spoke in my last book, Just for Today... 21 Day Devotional (shameless plug), wait is a verb. At this point, we know that time is our friend when it comes to process. We can either use it to grow us or we can use it to hinder us. Nevertheless, waiting is not the issue. How you wait is what usually messes us up. Suffering produces patience, which means while we suffer patience the fruit is being stirred up within us. Yet, we must remain positive even in the pain we bear. We can wait, but how we wait is what produces progress. As the title of this chapter says, processing is progress as long as we remain positive about it. I am not saying you will not have bad days. Bad days are common but it's how we manage the bad days. I suffered with bad anxiety after losing my ex-husband, the father of my children. I was having a lot of bad days. Most days I would just cry in the morning and declare that I would get through that day but some days I was panicking. Especially around Christmas time. When he was alive the majority of the Christmas gifts were from him. I rarely had to deal with getting big gifts because he would come through. The kids would each get a pair of Nike, some clothes, and the top thing on their list. However, this year I was having a rough time trying to figure out where to start. Plus, at the time, I was going through a whole attack on my finances. Kathy said to me on a girlfriend outing, "Ma'am, trust God. Everything will work out." God being God allowed all 4 of my parents to basically take care of 99.9% of the list the kids had. When I say I was so relieved and grateful. If I had just remained positive I probably wouldn't have had that argument with a client at work, that argument with my significant other, that argument with my mother and I wouldn't have had those sleepless nights.

Being positive is not being fake, however, it is speaking life over your circumstances. If you want to use the "fake it till you make it" saying, then so be it. But, the words that we speak are imperative when we are going through. David said in Psalms 39:1, "I will guard my ways, Lest I sin with my tongue; I will restrain my mouth with a muzzle, While the wicked are before me." I used to make a joke with my friends that I was praying for a muzzle for when they would say something off the wall to their spouses. Now I find myself truly praying for a muzzle for myself because one thing the enemy wants you to do, is to talk yourself out of your blessing. The elders used to say if you don't have anything nice to say then don't say it at all. They were wise in saying this. This is definitely a principle that needs to be embedded into our lives. Putting your mouth on a situation can actually mess up your breakthrough. I struggled with this for years. My uncle would always say, "Saying nothing doesn't make you a loser, Dominique." Of course, at the time I would say, "Well, I am not a loser." Clearly, I was because I just had to have the last word.

Chapter 7

Where is Everyone?

Processing can be very difficult sometimes. Sometimes you have to walk away from the things that you deeply want to stay. Other times you have to stay at things you want to walk away from. I must admit because I suffer from abandonment and rejection issues I am always tested at letting go of things. It always becomes super hard especially when you have history or even care for this person or situation. Recently, I had to walk away from a 25-year-old friendship. When I say I toiled and cried with it I was so torn up about it. I am sure that He thought that I was being extra or even just super emotional but deep down, I had enough of trying with this friendship. This friendship was causing me emotional pain. This was a friendship that I had for at least 25 years. We practically grew up together. We considered each other brother and sister but lately, it had taken a turn or so I thought. For the past few months, we had become closer and were hanging out a little more than normal. However, He was going through his own situation and I was finally out of my drama and looking forward to more. I was ready to try again, maybe even date again. I was excited to at least see what was out there. I figured since we were hanging out a little more why not see where this friendship could go? He was acting like a husband. I mean from the courting to spending time with my children it was a plus. I just knew this was it. I mean why not have such a love story where we were looking in all the wrong areas but it was right in front of us? I just knew this could be the one. Yet, I was fooled.

He was not ready at all. He was a great guy but he was emotionally broken. I am not sure if he knew what He was doing but it just became a headache. I felt so confused after being around him that I just now wanted to hate him and never be around him again. I never felt this way except with my ex-husband. The only issue was this was a good friend. I knew I had to walk away and finally be okay with it not working out but now our friendship was damaged. I was so hurt by the mixed signals he was sending and I really wanted to believe that He was not doing this on purpose but for some reason, I just couldn't settle with not holding him accountable. He was hurting me deeply. We would have these conversations of marriage, family, building, to have him end it with a simple phrase that basically said He was not interested in me. So, my conversation was great, my actions were great but I was left feeling still rejected. I finally had to tell myself, Nah, I'm good. This was not for me. I had to walk away even though I had promised Him I was here until the end. While deep down I wanted to be at the same time trying to be here would feel like a waste of time because He basically didn't want me around anyways.

It had become worse once my husband had passed away. He was more emotional than I was about him passing away. All I know is that this friendship was coming to a close. I was good on the extra weight.

I wish I could tell you that after you go through everything you will still have the same connections that have been there for years. Well, it's not likely that you will still have the same quantity but I can guarantee that the quality will be more. I used to be so sad that I was losing people like a 5-year-old loses their baby teeth. It was one after another. However, just like a kid, I was so focused on the fact that the teeth I was losing were fragile and not able to help me chew through some thick meat that was about to come my way. This is not to say that the connections that I lost were all horrible people. They just weren't on the same road I was traveling. Even if they were semi, we still had two different destinations.

One particular friendship that went through a transition during my season of pruning was actually more painful than the fact I was losing a husband. This friendship to me was a ride-or-die friendship. We were going through some similar issues yet we were handling it differently or so I thought. I believe I was just maybe a few months later in the process than what the person was. We went through some crazy moments in our years of being friends. However, this last situation left us not speaking for longer than normal. I think due to the fact we both were dealing with transitions in our lives that we both just didn't know how to deal with the other. I can only speak from my point of view and my point of view left me broken. Losing anyone can be painful but nobody ever talks about the heartbreak you feel when you lose a friend. Of course, from my brokenness viewpoint at the time, I thought that the person should have reached out due to the fact that I too was dealing with a divorce. Nevertheless, now that I am in a different space I know it was really miscommunication and to be honest we both were going through something.

Now that I look at it, neither one of us could have helped each other because we both were broken. We both were bruised. We both were trying to find our place in life. We both were trying to figure out what would happen after the divorce. We both were trying to figure out this new norm. To top it off, we were learning this new norm in the middle of a pandemic. Yet at that moment, I felt abandoned. I felt that I was left to go through this process alone. I didn't understand why God allowed so much loss to happen to me all at once but now that I am where I am, I am grateful.

Going through this alone stage helped me to learn what it meant when people said "Jesus is the best friend I ever had." I literally made Jesus my best friend. I would share my true feelings with Him and wouldn't hold back like I normally would with other friendships. I was able to really express what was hurting me, what I hated about the process, what I hated about myself at the moment, and what I hated about other people. Heck, I expressed to Him what I did not like that He was doing to me. The best part about it all was that Jesus never changed His love for me. Due to my suffering with abandonment and rejection issues, I always thought that if I ever shared my true feelings the friends I had would leave or reject me. Yet, the more mature I became I realized that people who couldn't love me for me were not who I needed around. I needed people who genuinely loved Dominique and not because of what she could give to them, help them, perform for them, or pray with and for them. I am not saying that all the people who were around me before the transition were like that, however, a transition requires loss. Who they became friends with before was no longer the same person. It takes strength and patience to remain friends with someone in the middle of a transition. Any transition whether it be marriage, divorce, birth, death, moving, etc. people change. Who I ever was, was not who I was and actually even now it's not who I am.

Being alone sometimes caused me to feel lonely and to be honest, I still feel that some days. Nonetheless, I am reminded that just because I am alone I am never lonely. Isaiah 41:10 says, *"So do not fear, for I am with you; do not be dismayed, for I am your God. I will strengthen you and help you; I will uphold you with my righteous right hand."* Being alone allowed me to really work on myself during my transition.

I remember one night I was sitting in my dining room with a good friend and we were talking about not realizing who we really had in our circle. Being alone allowed me to really observe who I had around me. For so long I would cry about the lack of help I was receiving from my children's father when it came to raising our children or even cry about the lack of support I had from my own father. It wasn't until that night I realized that my kids were tremendously blessed with a whole village that they actually lacked nothing. Even with myself, it wasn't until that conversation that I realized who God placed in my life. I longed for years to have a deeper relationship with my father but the older I became the more I became closed off to the idea. However, the more I became close to God the more my seeking subsided because He was supplying the need. Yet, at the same time He opened my eyes to the father figures I had around such as my uncle, Deek, my surrogate dad, Chris, my bonus father, Rodney, and my spiritual father/pastor, Bishop C. Guy Robinson. With all four of them, I knew that the scriptures

Psalms 27:10 and Psalms 68:5-6 were brought to life to me. God, the Father literally took care of me and then He placed me in families where I never lacked a father.

As I go back to the conversation, my good friend also let God use him with healing my abandonment issues. At a point in my life, I would always say that the only person who never dropped me as a man was my uncle. Until that night of having one of our many *"come to Jesus"* talks he reminded me that these people never dropped me. Yet, those moments when I expected them to be where I wanted them to be and they decided not to show up were not them dropping me. That was them not agreeing or co-signing to the drama that I had placed myself in. They weren't going to co-sign to the mess I was involving myself in. So many times we think that when people don't show that it's them not loving or supporting us or that they are rejecting us. I am here to tell you that this is not always the case. Many times we don't show up for people because we are not in agreement with what they are doing in their lives at the moment, especially if this is hindering them from becoming all God has destined them to be. If these people genuinely love, care, and support you they will not want to be around when you are damaging and self-sabotaging. Now that I am a more mature person, I heard that in a different light. It's not that they love me any less, they actually love me enough to not show up and cosign to my mess. These are the types of people you will want to acquire when you are transiting because these people will hold you accountable for who God says you are and not what your circumstance says. I am now grateful for the people who decided not to show up when I was in the mess I was in. Deep down their tough love for me helped pull me through; even if it was to show them at the time that I didn't need them. Nevertheless, we are not independent people, we are interdependent people. Meaning we can never just do life on our own, but who we have around us, praying for us, and even those who love us from afar are actually all a part of the plan that God has predestined for us. So, to answer the question that was proposed in the beginning, "Where Is Everyone?," they are exactly where they need to be. Whether that's not in your circle or your circle, loving, praying, and supporting you from afar or close to you. These individuals are exactly where they are supposed to be. The real question is, "Are you where you are supposed to be?"

Chapter 8

SpinnaBlock

I know this chapter title is so hilarious. I have to credit it to my good friend, Minister Daniel Curtis. We were having a conversation about a project I wanted to pursue. He told me that he would get some information for me and when he finally got it that he would "spinnablock." For those of you who don't know what it means, it simply means that you will return with vengeance to complete what you started. After he said that to me it became my declaration for a month. I was making jokes with my friends saying that Jesus was about to SpinnaBlock for me. Meaning everything that I thought I lost or mismanaged, Jesus was about to give me another chance to get it right. Little did I know Jesus actually did exactly what I was declaring. Now was I ready for Him to "SpinnaBlock" was the question. Well, for starters I did not think He would actually do it. I guess that goes back to what the season people would say, "Be careful what you pray for." God began to give me little by little things that I prayed for in one season that I either mismanaged or lost. First, it was my old job. When I was at this job before I was mismanaging the time I had that I could actually work and pursue my business dreams. At the time I was here the first time I was so focused on dating and entertaining this toxic relationship that I didn't actually heal from the divorce I was dealing with at the time. However, this go around I was more interested in building my business from the ground up again and I was begging God to allow me to be creative again. Once I started the job and had my own office I was back to feeling excited to create. I began doing what I used to do and building and writing ideas down. I began to plan out a retreat and that's when I realized that my creativity was back. My desire to build was back.

Later God started to restore other parts of my life and then one day in the middle of my restoration process I had a mental breakdown. You would think that I would be content with what God was doing but nope not me. I wanted things to go my way. I wanted the relationship God was restoring to go my way, my friendships to go my way and my business progress to go my way. Yet, God was not having it. It was either I followed His way or I was going to experience unnecessary struggle in every area God was trying to restore. Have you ever felt like that? Like you were given a dream, a vision, or a promise and you begin to obsess over making sure that things went well with it. Yup, that was me. I became obsessive over the promises God gave me. I was in a tug of war with myself. The spiritual side wanted to follow Jesus but the natural side wanted to make sure we didn't fail again. I was so used to feeling like a failure that when I was actually winning spiritually I was still failing mentally and emotionally. I wanted my wins to be physical because that's what I saw. I saw the world winning. I saw the world happy on social media in love with their partner, traveling and building businesses that were making great money. Well, at least that's what they portrayed. I was reminded one morning after my breakdown that scripture says, "Whoever believes in Him (*meaning Jesus*) will not be put to shame." (Romans 10:11) one thing I experienced a lot was shame. Shame is defined by Google as a painful feeling of humiliation or distress caused by the consciousness of wrong or foolish behavior. Biblically it represents a defeated or degraded state. The Greek word for shame in that scripture is kataischuno. It means to curse vehemently, put to utter confusion, or frustrate. I realized that every time I put my trust in myself I felt ashamed which means that I was doing life wrong. If shame was my portion for putting trust in myself that meant I needed to trust in something better that would not cause humiliation, confusion, or frustration. That something better was and is Jesus. I realize that if I wholeheartedly believe in Him and not just His promises but Him that He would not put me to shame. I would not be disappointed if I confidently believed in Jesus. My great friend told me this morning on my way to work that this was the season for me to get my confidence back but the only way I could get it back is if I confidently believed that Jesus was my savior. In order for God to truly spinnablock for me I had to truly spinnablock for Him. Today, I make a full decision to fully trust in Jesus with no doubt because I know that He would never have me confused and humiliated. For He said in Isaiah 54:4, "Do not fear, for you will not be put to shame, And do not feel humiliated *or* ashamed, for you will not be disgraced. For you will forget the shame of your youth, And you will no longer remember the disgrace of your widowhood," and in Isaiah 28:16, "Because of these things, this is what the Lord God says: 'I will put a stone in the ground in Jerusalem. This will be a tested stone. Everything will be built on this important and precious rock. Anyone who trusts in it will never be disappointed.'" Yet my favorite is the promise that He gave to us who have dealt with shame in Isaiah 61:7, "Instead of your shame you shall have double honor, And instead of confusion, they shall rejoice in their portion. Therefore in their land they shall possess double; Everlasting joy shall be theirs." Maybe you are like me and have felt like a disgrace in life or a bit confused about why things are not working in your favor. Or maybe after dealing with so much pain and hurt you begin to doubt the very thing that God promised you because it doesn't look like what everyone else looks like. I am here to remind you that you must hold on because the pain will end. Not only will the pain end but you shall receive double for your trouble.

Chapter 9

Introduction

I know many of you are confused about why the introduction is at the end of the book. Many books have an introduction in the beginning. However, due to me finally knowing who I am and what I am supposed to do, I realized that introducing myself after you read through the process would make my introduction more important at the end of this book than at the beginning. Especially being that this was really the beginning of a new life.

So, as Sean 'Jay-Z' Carter says, "Allow me to re-introduce myself." Hello, everyone, my name is Dominique Farmer better known as Victorious, Healed, Daughter of The King Jesus Christ. I am the mother of 2 beautiful children, Jelani Michaela and Jonathan Patrick, II. I was a victim of Domestic Violence, Abandonment, and Rejection, BUT God! I am now a daughter full of hope and ready to help my sisters in Christ get through what I've gone through. I am an author. I am the owner of *And She Lived, Inc.* a foundation that helps women & children through the transitions of life from being a victim of Domestic Violence and/or Divorce to becoming victorious women. I have other businesses that I manage as God provides but they are still in the works. And I am a preacher of the Gospel and I am finally okay with being known as Minister Dominique Farmer.

I was going to name this chapter, "Say Yes" but I thought making it an introduction shows that I finally said 'Yes' to my purpose. It was like an "Ah Ha" moment when I realized what exactly I was supposed to do. I mean after all the pain I knew some type of purpose had to come out of it. If there was nothing else I held onto, I held on to the hope that God would finally give me what I desired, especially dealing with all that I've dealt with. After dealing with rejection and abandonment from almost every male in my life, betrayal from family members and close friends, domestic violence with my ex-husband, and almost committing suicide about 5 times, I, for sure knew God had more to my story. Heck, Jesus' story didn't end at death, so I knew mine wouldn't either.

I knew that if I held on then soon enough pain would end. Now do I believe that I will never have pain in my life again? Absolutely not, but I do know that I will not feel that type of pain again. Not because it wouldn't come back to me and try me again but because I was a different person. I had boundaries now, I lived to a certain standard, I knew I wasn't that little broken girl anymore and most importantly, I knew who I was and who I belonged to. I knew that being an intercessor wasn't just to intercede for others but also to intercede for myself. God had so graciously given me many gifts but for so long I sucked at stewarding those gifts in the way He gave them to me. God blesses us with gifts to edify the Kingdom. Last I checked I, too, am a part of this kingdom. Which meant that I was to also be a giver, intercede, show forgiveness, and show unconditional love not just to others but to myself. I had to pour into myself just as much, if not twice as much as I did for everyone else. I had to stop and pray for myself just as much as I called my friends and prayed for them in the middle of the day. I had to forgive myself just as much as I forgave others. I had to give to myself just as much as I gave to others. I had to clap for myself as much as I clap for others. I had to honor myself just as much as I honored others. Not only did I have to do all of that, I had to get out of my own way so that I could grow into what God had predestined me to be. I wanted to finally be the woman God saw and be strong enough to carry the weight that He had for me.

    I don't mean weight that will crush you but I mean the weight of His glory. I want His glory to sit on me as He did with the disciples in Acts 2 that afterward gave them the power to do the unexplainable, power that allowed them to say I don't know how but I know who. Being under His glory comes with weight! Saying Yes comes with weight. However, it also comes with the strength of who you said yes to. I believe that what God was doing through my life was to finally get me here to fully submit to what He had. However, because I was so broken and lived as an orphan, I just couldn't submit to another "man." But it was in my brokenness that I learned He wasn't a man. He was exactly who I needed at the time. Whether it was a mother, a father, a friend, a lover, a doctor, a creator, a provider, or a lawyer, He was whatever I needed Him to be. "I am that I am" was exactly that to me.

So, again, I am because He was, is, and shall be. I am able to live without the pains of rejection, abandonment, and/or violence because of His blessing, His breaking, and His healing. Just like Jesus did at the communion table, He blessed me, He broke me, and now He is ready to pass me out to bless and fulfill His assignment on the earth. This is just the beginning. Hold on, Pain Ends, and Your Purpose Begins.

Bonus Chapter

It's Time for WAR!

I thought I was done writing but the Lord had me write this last chapter because many of us have to actually war for our joy to be returned. I had finally caught a break and I thought I was actually finally in a season of happiness. I was up one Saturday night praying through the night and once I finished praying I looked at the time and saw 12:22 am. At the time I heard the Spirit of God say, "It's your time!" I became excited but I just simply went to sleep because I had church in the morning. While at church the Spirit was heavy in there and my pastor prophetically announced that it was "Our Time for Supernatural Favor." So, I was led to sow but I only had $12 in my cash app to give. So, I gave that above my tithes and offerings. I sent my seed and wrote in the notes "Manifest." That Wednesday, my son became sick and I decided to stay at home with him. While home I was enjoying some time and I received a call from my job offering me a promotion for a new position. This position included a 12% raise. I first was going to pass up but everyone was telling me to take it. I wasn't expecting it because at the time I was comfortable at my job. I was able to work and chill. So, I accepted the position. I was so excited to see that $12 turn into 12% so I testified of the goodness of God to my Pastor who had me testify in front of the church. I knew that everything would be okay. A few days later someone from my office who shall remain nameless came to me telling me that the HR office had messed up and offered the position that was supposed to be mine to another person as well. I became a bit nervous but I didn't let it bother me because I did not hear anything opposite of what was first told to me over the phone and via email. Two weeks later it was time for me to begin my onboarding process and transfer so I called the lady who offered me the position to confirm everything. She was a bit hesitant but confirmed that I was still on to start on November 29th. An hour passed and she called me back apologizing and saying that they had to rescind the offer. I remained calm on the phone with her and requested to speak with a supervisor. As I waited for the supervisor's call I closed my office door and began to weep to Jehovah Gibbor. I was determined that God was not a man who gives gifts and then takes them away. While I do know God gives and He takes but this promotion was not something I even asked for. God is a good father so I knew that this was definitely a trick of the enemy. I finally spoke to the supervisor but this person was very rude. That day I prayed and cried all day until I spoke with my friend who lit a fire under me. She said, "Ma'am, it's time you do your midnight prayers." At first, I felt like midnight prayers were a sacrifice that I was not willing to make. However, I had enough of the enemy fighting me and taking my confidence. If anything I was willing to try it and gain an ounce of confidence. That day I started writing scriptures I planned to take to war with me and I called my mother who was willing to go to battle with me. That night was life-changing. I had never prayed like that before. I felt that God had given me confidence in a way that I had never experienced. I felt bold to walk into the enemy's camp and take back by force what was mine. That night I took back my boldness, I took back my faith, and I took back my strength that allowed the enemy to just take with no fight. While I was there I took back a few other things. I was grateful that I was willing to go to war with the enemy because many days I would just let the enemy take and I would not fight back. However, this time around I had become annoyed with letting the enemy just steal and kill my joy. It was time to stop moving from a place of fighting for victory and reminding myself that I already had victory. I loved how Revelation 12:12 says, "Therefore rejoice, O heavens, and you who dwell in them! Woe to the inhabitants of the earth and the sea! For the devil has come down to you, having great wrath, because he knows that he has a short time."

The enemy knows his time is almost up so why not try to bring people with him? Yet, I refused to be one of them. Those midnight prayer calls with my mother started something for me. It gave me not just confidence but it gave me a better relationship with my mother on a different level. I grew up hearing my grandmother pray but not my mother so much. Hearing my mother war in such a subtle way gave me so much joy. I have gained so much from those few days of midnight prayer. I have gained boldness, confidence, more faith, and a deeper relationship with Jesus and my mother. I am truly grateful that my friend gave me this assignment because I would not be so sure that God is truly fighting on my behalf as I do my part. God gave us authority according to 2 Corinthians 10:4 to pull down strongholds, casting down arguments and every high thing that exalts itself against the knowledge of God, bringing every thought into captivity to the obedience of Christ. I was over letting the enemy beat me up and I just took it.

One thing led to another and I found myself searching and really diving deep into the things of God. I found myself watching a video of the lovely Prophetess Tiphani Montgomery and she had just begun a new fast called the Year of The Bride Fast. While in my mind this had nothing to do with my finances but I was led to actually follow her lead in this fast. I began the fast on November 27th, which happened to be my son's birthday and it ended on December 21st, the day before my birthday. I believe if I had not done this fast that I would not have known so much that God was trying to do to me. Because of the Fast and her nightly teachings, I would have never really known about the different covenants that I had to break before God was going to release what He had for me including the promotion. Scripture says in Hosea 4:6 that people are destroyed for lack of knowledge. I was allowing my lack of knowledge of the things of God to destroy my future but Thank God for grace and mercy. If that promotion had never been rescinded I would have never known to break the covenant I made with Moloch unknowingly that kept aborting everything that I put my hands to. I had a spirit of not finishing because that covenant had a legal right to harass me. BUT GOD! Once I began to study and watch Prophetess Tiphani about breaking covenants and replacing them with the New Covenant with Jesus Christ I would have never been able to take legal action with the blood and use my legal right to take back what belongs to me without retaliation. I was doing what Jeremiah 33:3 says, "Call unto me, and I will answer thee, and show thee great and mighty things, which thou knowest not." I became a new creature and I was finally walking out my faith.

Then something happened. In the middle of my fast, I received a call to come and interview for the position they rescinded and tried to replace the offer with. I went to the interview and I like to believe that I threw it out of the park. Normally they tell you within 2-3 weeks if you received the job but I received a call on that Monday after the interview which was on that Thursday that I received the job. I was excited but I decided this time that I would keep it quiet until I was in my new position and then I would tell my full testimony. However, just to know that I was able to wave the banner of victory with the help of the Holy Ghost that this was truly something that I needed to see.

Many times we give up in the middle of the fight which allows the enemy to beat up on us. Maybe that may not be your story but if you are anything like me, I would quit fighting in the middle with the enemy because I just felt like he was winning. Nevertheless, this time I was determined to see the end of the fight. Growing up as the person who would fight all the time I had to use that same energy I had fighting people to fight the enemy. As a young girl, I would make sure I won the fight because I was determined to beat the person who kept messing with me. Yet as I got older I became a punk and let the enemy beat up on me for years. But I vowed that moving forward I was not going to just sit there and let the enemy beat up on me anymore. Especially being that I made a covenant with Jesus Christ. I was guaranteed a win because Jesus already said I had the victory.

Moving forward I want to leave you with this commandment. Never let the enemy beat you up. If your situation doesn't look like what God spoke over your life then keep fighting, keep praying, keep praising, and keep worshiping until what you see looks like what God said. It may get hard. It may get darker but be reminded that *"the sufferings of this present time are not worth comparing with the glory that is to be revealed to us."* (Romans 8:18)

God has a new name for you. Isaiah 62:4 says, "Thou shalt no more be termed Forsaken; neither shall thy land any more be termed Desolate: but thou shalt be called Hephzibah, and thy land Beulah: for the Lord delighteth in thee, and thy land shall be married." God wants to take you from Forsaken to Hephzibah. Hephzibah in Greek means "my delight is in her." Many of us started this book in a broken place but I declare that when you finish this book you will end with a New Name. Maybe you started this being hurt but you will end Healed. Broken to Blessed. Poverty to Prosperity. Single to Married. God has a land called Beulah with your name on it. While Beulah means married but when a marriage begins it starts with a celebration. I believe that this will be your season of celebration! Let's celebrate because the war is over and YOU HAVE WON!

Acknowledgments

First giving honor to Jesus Christ. It is really Him that I live, move and have my being. I am because of Him. I am forever grateful that Jesus chose someone like me to fulfill His mission on earth.

I want to acknowledge my beautiful children, Jelani & Jonathan II. Thank you for allowing me to grow and become a better person while raising such amazing people like you. Thank you for being so patient with me.

Dad & Momma Lisa, thank you for being patient with me as we grow in grace to a better and healthy relationship. Dad, I love you! Thank you so much!

Pah & Mommy, thank you for everything. You rock and I am so grateful that I have you guys in my life.

To my Wingate crew, Gram, Uncle Deek, Aunt Dawn, Azariah, and JD, thank you for letting me take ya'll to my therapy session after each movie we watch.

To my sissy, Kathy, I am so grateful that God allowed our paths to cross and the impact you have in my life. I am grateful that God allowed me to learn and develop what Godly friendship is with you. I appreciate you ever so much.

Last but certainly not least to my Tabernacle (The TOTLC) Family, I LOVE YOU! My spiritual parents, Bishop C. Guy & Minister Sandra Robinson have truly been there to watch me grow and mature into who I am today. Thank you for accepting me and also assisting me with my maturation process in the spirit and physically. Thank you so much Pastor-Dad and my Naomi.

I would be remiss if I didn't acknowledge you, the reader, for purchasing and reading this. I pray that you are blessed and I pray that you have an encounter with Jesus Christ that will change your life in a way that is unexplainable. I pray that every pain, hurt, and discomfort that you have ever experienced will turn one day into purpose. As I close, be reminded that "All things work together for good to those who love God, to those who are the called according to His purpose." (Romans 8:28, NKJV)

About the Author

Dominique C. Farmer is a mother, licensed minister, minister of arts through dance, serial entrepreneur, author, and so many other titles.

Dominique was licensed as a Minister in November 2019, under the direction of Bishop C. Guy Robinson of the Tabernacle of the Lord Church & Ministries.

Dominique received her education in the Baltimore City Public School System attending the Edmondson-Westside High School and the Community College of Baltimore County. She enrolled in Liberty University pursuing a degree in Theology and Biblical Studies.

Author of "Just for Today... 21 Day Devotional," Dominique is an advocate of free will praise. She believes that you can praise the Lord wherever you are and in various forms. In addition, Dominique is a firm believer of the WORD of GOD; specifically, as stated in Matthew 6:33 *"But seek ye first the kingdom of God and His righteousness and all things shall be added to you."* She lives, breathes, and demonstrates this verse in everything she does.

While Dominique enjoys praising the LORD, she also enjoys spending time with her daughter, Jelani, and son, Jonathan II, writing, preaching, and doing whatever she can for the LORD and His Kingdom.

Made in the USA
Middletown, DE
13 March 2024